More REFLECTIONS OF GLOSSOP

Model Farm and Cat Wood

FOXLINE
PUBLISHING

Margaret Buxton - Knott

Copyright © 1996 Foxline Publishing and Margaret Buxton - Knott
ISBN 1 870119 46 0
All rights reserved
Designed and Edited by BA Graphics
Typeset by Bill Rear.
Printed by the Amadeus Press, Huddersfield.

Published by Foxline Publishing
32, Urwick Road, Romiley, Stockport. SK6 3JS

AUTHORS NOTE

As the daughter of a well known local photographer. Harry Buxton, I have put together some more of his collection of interesting and historical photographs from Glossop life. The first book 'REFLECTIONS OF GLOSSOP' covered the period up to 1950. This book takes us up to 1974 when Glossop Borough Council was merged with High Peak. For many it was the end of an era.   *Margaret Buxton-Knott*

INTRODUCTION

Glossop is a town in Derbyshire, on the edge of the Peak District and just a few minutes drive from the Pennine Way. The A57 Snake Road marks a point on the Pennine Way between Shelf Moor and Featherbed Moss and follows the line of the Medieval Doctor's Gate which drops down through Woodlands Valley. Doctor's Gate was named after Doctor Talbot who rediscovered it. Growing out of a mill town, Glossop has developed into a tourist area, with the railway station bringing people from the cities to enjoy the open spaces of the surrounding countryside. The Tourist Information Centre in the Gatehouse on Victoria Street directs tourists to the places of interest and the Heritage Centre on Henry Street gives an insight into the historical development of Glossop.

DEDICATION

I dedicate this book to all who live or have lived in Glossop, and especially in memory of my father, Harry Buxton (Sept 1908-Jan 1983). As one of his work colleagues once said, "He was the Photographer of the Unexpected and never left home without a camera". He took and processed his first photograph when he was only seven years of age. During the war he served as a police photographer in Glossop, and was a member of the Borough Council in the early seventies. He gave many slide lectures and had a great interest in amateur and C. B. radio.

For details of price and availability ask your bookseller or send s.a.e to:
FOXLINE Publishing
32 Urwick Road ROMILEY
Stockport Cheshire SK6 3JS
Telephone   0161 430 6834

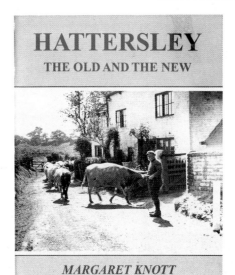

1950

The Grouse Inn, May 1950. The licensees at this time were Mr & Mrs Cyril Bradley and Rover, their dog, is seen at the door. The tree only bloomed on one side because of the strong winds that prevail here. Often snow used to block the road. Once a 17th century farmhouse the farmer, seeing a way to make extra cash, began brewing and selling his own beer and soon forgot farming. The North East Cheshire Drag Hunt used to leave from the Grouse Inn, which got its name from shooting but now only clay pigeons are shot. The Inn was still lit by oil lamps in 1950. In the early days, supplies used to arrive by horse when a gill of beer cost 1½p and a small rum cost 2d, It was a free house for many years until Walker & Humprays bought it the thirties. It had few motorists during the war due to petrol rationing. Some of the former licensees include Jim Hall, Joe Bennett, Mr Stephenson and Albert Pass. The latter kept the Inn for twenty years and was the first to get a Sunday extension. There is only one car in the carpark, but there were three million cars and lorries in Britaln by 1950

September 1950 Mossy Lea. 1000 sheep from the moors near the Snake Pass were rounded up by local farmers Mr Shepherd & Mr Wheeldon, for the annual sheep dipping. They were assisted by eight dogs and the operation took about three hours. It is near here that work on the Old Glossop section of Glossop Brook received £2.7 million for the flood prevention scheme in 1994, Stepped rocks have provided mini waterfalls along the river course from Mossy Lea to Manor Park to break down silt which was washed down to lower stretches of the river and caused flooding. To the right of this picture is the route to Doctor's Gate, In the 17th century, Glossop was reached from Derwent by this paved causeway over thick peat bog and was known as Doctor Talbot's Gate.

The Drovers Arms at the foot of Chunal Lane was formerly owned by Lord Howard and bought by Boddington's Brewery in 1925. It was the base for Glossop Rugby Club before it had its own headquarters. The Drover's got it's name from the men who used to drive their animals to market across the nearby moors. Up to seventy horses could be stabled at the pub, they carried coal to the mills and logs for the paper mill. From 1977 Charlie & Margaret Griffiths were the landlords Pictured here is Sandy the dog with Jim Hinchlifte, who is quite at home with a pint and his dominoes. It is now the base for High Peak MG Owners Club.

July 1951. £900 had been spent on the children's recreation ground in Manor Park and was opened for the second time by Alderman Robert Boak, who was the Mayor. The grounds of Glossop Hall had been opened to the public as Manor Park in 1927. The first Hall was built by Ralph Standish Howard in 1729 and demolished in 1850, it was known as The Royal Hall. The new hall was built by the 13th Duke of Norfolk in 1850-51. The aviary and pets corner was opened in the park in April 1955 and closed in 1994 to make way for a native trail.

November 1951. Happy at their work, the rat catchers at Whitfield They were George Gray & Richard Whittaker; Mr Dunsmore (Sanitary inspector) and an official from the Ministry of Agriculture & Fisheries. Every six months, rat poison was dropped down the town's 550 manholes. Rats have always followed man wherever he has built houses and towns. The house rat or black rat is smaller than the more common brown rat Both kinds escaped into Britain from Eastern ships in our ports. The brown rat is fond of water and travels through sewers. It is the black rat which spreads Bubonic plague A female rat can have up to eight litters a year with around 20 young in each litter, each of which can begin to breed after three months of age. Although owls, hawks and stoats prey on them, man wages continual war against them by poisoning. gassing and trapping Today modern poisons are more effective and painless, compared to older methods.

February 1952. English winters are certainly less severe than in the past. Here photographer Harry Buxton clears the snow from this road sign near North Road, to reveal the depth of the drift.

(Below - left)

Mrs Walsh of Charles Street kept this pet monkey, which was named Judy, even though he was male. He could eat with a spoon and slept in pyjamas!

1952

This Bush Baby, which belonged to Mr Lomas of Spire Hollin, escaped and was finally found on tile roof of a house in the town.

March 1952. The Rotary club collected useful items to aid Greece. Two tons of goods were loaded onto a lorry belonging to Volcrepe Limited en route to Athens. Italian troops had invaded Greece and been driven out in 1944 with the help of British Troops, prior to the Germans taking up occupation. Civil War against the Communists until 1949 caused much devastation. In 1952 Greece joined the U.S., Canada and the Western European nations in the defensive alliance called N.A.T.O (North Atlantic Treaty Organisation).

1952

April1952. 80 year old Wilfred Hall of North Road was the oldest blacksmith working part-time at J. Nield's in Manor Street off High Street East.

October 1952. A fallen tree blocked Slatelands Road at Bridgefield, off Primrose Lane. Bungalows now stand on the site of the garage. Bridgefield Mill once stood on the Gnat Hole Brook near the fallen tree. Primrose Mill was further down Primrose Lane, on the opposite side of the brook.

1952

1952. Ukrainians who came to the north of England during the second world war met at the Victoria hall to enjoy traditional dancing. The Ukraine, a republic of the USSR, was invaded and occupied by the Germans from 1941-44, and many of their factories were destroyed. They came to England to work in our cotton mills. At Christmas they all gathered to celebrate with St Nicholas and a black faced demon. The demon was supposed to clear the path for the saint to distribute gifts to the children.

July 1953. The fountain in front of the Norfolk Arms was crafted by David Williams from Wales around 1881. He also helped in the building of Dinting Church and Vicarage. It was given to the town by Mrs. Ann Wood, wife of the mill owning family from Whitfield House. She also paid for two other fountains on the corner of Manor Park Road/Sheffield Road and Victoria Street/St.Mary's Road. In the photograph, four year old Pat McMyler was looking at a fountain that didn't work. At the top is a tap for humans, below is a trough for horses and at the bottom a trough for dogs. In 1967 the council considered removing it, but fortunately it still stands and was restored to working order in July 1995.

September 1953. Joe Davis came to the Liberal Club on Henry Street to play against Bill Cumming at a celebrity snooker match. Joe stayed overnight in the Norfolk Arms. He was born at Whitwell, near Chesterfield, in 1901 and learned to play billiards by watching clients at his father's hotel. At the age of 12 he made his first break of 100 and in 1927 he won the world professional snooker championship and was never beaten until he retired in 1946. In 1928 he won the British Billiards Championship and held the title until 1933. In 1955 he made the maximum snooker break of 147 and this was recognised by the Billiards Association & Control Council as a world record two years later. He was awarded the OBE in 1963. His younger brother followed the same career and they are the only players to have won both the world billiards and snooker championships. Joe Davis died in 1978. Glossop Liberal Club was once the headquarters of Oswald Partington, who was MP for the High Peak in 1910. It is now a theatre for the Partington Players. His foundation stone was laid by Sir Edward Partington (Lord Doverdale) in 1914 and the club was named in 1957.

1953

October 1953. Ex-members of the 8th Army: Alfred Leney, Maurice Mollart, George Midgley, Donald Robinson, Fred Gregary, Emrys Evans, Walter Swann, Jimmy Cuthbert and Alan Dewsnap from Glossop and Longdendale, were welcomed to the Empire Cinema, on High Street West, by the manager and the Mayor, Richard Beckmann. The men, who had all served in the Middle East, were reunited to watch the film 'The Desert Rats' at the invitation of the manager.

1954

May 1954. Sir John Barbirolli conducted the Hallé Orchestra in rehearsal for a concert held in the Victoria Hall. Born in London in 1899 of French and Italian parents, he was a cello player and in 1937 succeeded Toscanini as conductor of the New York Philharmonic. He returned to England and conducted the Hallé in Manchester from about 1943. The Hallé was formed by Sir Charles Hallé, a German born pianist and conductor who had settled in Manchester after the Revolution of 1848. He died in 1895. Under Barbirolli the orchestra became amongst the finest in the world. He married an oboist in 1939, was awarded the gold medal of the Royal Philharmonic Society in 1950 and given the Freedom of Manchester in 1958.

July 1954. This model railway layout, by Robin Sidebottom, John Neal, Lesley Wood and John Lawton, was on display at an Arts, Crafts and Hobbies exhibition at Glossop Grammar School on Talbot Street. The school was here until the new school opened in September 1959 on Talbot Road. This building became the home of the Community College.

1954. This was the scene at the Cooperative slaughter-house at the end of food rationing. Rationing had started in 1940, due to war time shortages. In January 1950 the bacon ration was increased from 4 to 5 ounces a week per person, but by April it was reduced again. By the summer the meat ration was increased but tea was reduced. One year before the end of rationing an American chemist, Robert Boyer, patented a bland tasting meat substitute from the protein rich remains of Soya beans, but as this didn't become available until 1960 it had no effect on meat rationing in the 1950's. The Glossopdale New Industrial Cooperative Society was established in 1866, with registered offices in Railway Street and branches in High Street West from 1877 and in Whitfield from 1882. These stores had various departments including grocery, drapery, boot, shoe and clog, coal, education and a library.

1954

October 16 1954. The Duke of Devonshire opened Red Court's home for the mentally handicapped. Officially known as Devonshire House after the Duke, it was the last home of Edward Partington who became Lord Doverdale. In 1960 an extension, Derby House, was opened by Lord Derby and in 1968 a second extension, Alexandra House, was opened by princess Alexandra.

October 1954. The Superintendent of Belle Vue Zoo, Gerald Iles, came to the Town Hall with some of his pets to entertain members of the Music Club. The thrill of the evening was when he showed this Royal Python from West Africa. He walked round the audience to allow them to touch and prove for themselves that snakes are not slimy things. The author of this book, who was sitting in the audience, asked Mr Iles if she could have the snake around her neck. She was duly led to the stage and posed for this picture. Later, Mr Iles wrote a book called 'At Home in the Zoo' about the history of Belle Vue Zoo and this photograph appeared on the fly leaf.

1954

November 1954. These German war medals were on show at a Rotary Club meeting in the Norfolk Arms. The medal at the bottom left with the swastika was the 'Mother's Cross' which was awarded to German mothers who had five or more children.

1955

November 1955. Mr Jesse Pass was a local artist from Castle Hill in Old Glossop and had a cobbler's shop on High Street East. In February 1961 Mr Pass had a water-colour of All Saints Church accepted by the Manchester Academy of Fine Arts, and it was hung at the Spring exhibition.

November 1955. Alf Oldham, the licensee of the Rose & Crown on High Street West. The pub was built c.1650. Sir John Barbirolli visited in 1947 when a fellow music lover, Alfred Scragg, was the licensee. Rossini and Liszt were often played in the public bar. The Oddfellows and Foresters used the upper room as their headquarters. Some who have served behind the bar include Messrs. Collier, Mayhew, Bridge, Farnworth, Birch, Hayes and Locking. When Mike and Valerie Dash took over in 1978, they installed a fountain in the lounge bar to collect money for charity. Here in 1955 a pile of pennies, on the top of a beer glass, was collected to help the Old Folk's Welfare Committee. This committee was set up in 1949 when Councillor Higton was the Mayor. Old Folks' Week was an annual event held in October, where special events were held to raise money to help the older residents. In the early 1940's the Rotary Club founded the Old Men's Corner and the Hundred Club. The Community House on Market Street was opened as an Old People's Centre in October 1957. The first opening of the building had been in 1933 when Mrs. M.L. Casey, a former mayor, was the opener with the current mayor, Councillor C. Woolley opening the Old Folks' Week. Mrs. E. Higton (Secretary) and Mrs. Goodwright (Treasurer) headed the committee which brought the scheme to fruition for this opening in 1957. Women using the building had formed the Friday Club in 1953 and their choir sang 'Bless This House' at the opening. The Building was demolished in 1994 and replaced by Bradbury House, a new centre for the community. It was officially opened by Lady Hilton in October 1995.

February 1956. The severe temperatures caused this horse and cattle trough to freeze. It was on Dinting Vale near to Simmondley Lane. These two eight year olds, Peter Bates and Vera Dalton, looked on at the scene.

1956

May 1956. This bus crashed into the back of a three ton lorry on Chunal Lane as it was taking workers from Strines Print Works back to their homes in Glossop and Hadfield. The red brick building at Strines belonged to English Calico Ltd., on the banks of the River Goyt on the Cheshire/Derbyshire border. Two men at the company used to produce a monthly journal for the workers in the mid 1800's. It was a topical journal of science and art and contained only pleasant matters, neither referring to contentious issues within the work place, such as wages, hours and holidays.

1957

February 1957. It was announced that the Arundel Street Gas Works was to close down and the site demolished. It had been originally founded by the Duke of Norfolk in 1845, with the sum of £6,000 in £10 shares. The shareholders held their first meeting in the Town Hall and were known as the Glossop Gas Light Company. Good dividends were paid right up to nationalisation in 1949. The British Gas Corporation was privatised in 1986. In Glossop gas produced at the local gas works was used to light the local mills and from 1861 the street lamps were powered by gas, before being lit by electricity from 1945. In 1995 the new Kwik Save store was built on the site of the Gas Works.

March 1957. High Street West with the Gas Works chimney over the café sign. Wren Nest Mill (formerly Sumner' Mill) can be seen in the distance. Swire & Sons shoe shop is on the right next to the Co-operative Society. Car parking was allowed on the left hand side of the road but there was No Waiting between 8am and 10pm on the other side.

August 1957. There have been many accidents on the A57 Snake Road. This 7 ton 60 feet long articulated RAF lorry crashed through the wall at Brook Bank Corner, rolling down 100 feet into the rock strewn gulley below. The driver managed to jump clear. In 1994 the Derbyshire County Council and Peak Park Planning Board conducted a road traffic survey which revealed that the people of Glossop are suffering from heavy traffic passing through the town en route from Manchester to Sheffield. In 1993 the daily average of traffic using the Snake Pass was 4,250 vehicles. By 1994 this had increased to 4,600, with 360 of these additional vehicles being lorries.

July 1957. The scene of the collision between a Ford car and a bus in High Street West, near Sumner's Mill. Although trapped, the driver was not killed. It was during this year that the Clean Air Act gave the local authorities the power to create smoke control areas. Grants of 70% were available to adapt stoves and grates to using smokeless fuel. Houses like these all had coal fires and their close proximity added to the air pollution.

August 1957. This row of four houses and two shops in Victoria Street were being demolished after standing empty for some time, due to bulging walls. The buildings had been known as 'shivering row' since being struck by lightening in 1962. The top shop was Pownall's before it moved premises to High Street East. The Town Hall clock is just visible between the chimneys.

1957

October 1957. The 11th Duke of Devonshire, Andrew Robert Buxton Cavendish, opened the Grammar School's two day bazaar, held to boost the school's amenities fund. The Duke is seen here with school governor Mrs Lawton, buying chocolates from one of the stalls. At the time the Duke lived at Edensor House and did not move into Chatsworth House until 1959. He was Mayor of Buxton from 1952-54. The 1st Earl of Devonshire was the son of Sir William Cavendish and Bess of Hardwick. The 4th Earl was created 1st Duke of Devonshire in 1694. The 11th Duke's heir is Perigrine Cavendish, Marquis of Hartington.

November 1957. Alderman Joseph Doyle was made a Freeman of Glossop, in recognition of his eminent service to the town. He was the seventh Freeman and the only one living at the time. The first was Edward Partington. The other Freemen of the Borough were Ann Kershaw-Wood, Isaac Jackson, Harriet Jackson, Alice Partington, Alfred J. Law, Robert J. Boak and Harry Cooper. The Mayor, Claude Woolley, is seen here handing over the certificate in the presence of Town Clerk P. Campbell, in the Council Chambers. The Glossop Coat of Arms, seen in the Council Chamber, has the motto VIRTUS VERITAS LIBERTAS meaning "For Moral Perfection, Truth and Freedom". It had always been the school badge of the Grammar School.

1957. Norfolk Square. At this time the paths across formed a diagonal route. The carpet garden shows it was the Jubilee of the Scouting Movement, started by Robert Baden Powell when he organised boys to help the army during the Boer War in South Africa when Mafeking was besieged. Back in Britain he wrote his ideas in "Scouting for Boys". Today there are over 16 million scouts in more than 150 countries. The square was once known as Norfolk Garden. The lawn and trees in the square were financed after the first world war, by Mrs. Bennett Sidebottom, a daughter of Lord Doverdale. In May 1995 the square underwent a £250,000 facelift and won first prize in the Derbyshire County Council Greenwatch Awards.

January 1958. Neil Walton with early lambs at his father's farm in Dinting.

1958

(below - left)

May 1958. Norfolk Square. The carpet garden was laid out to herald the visit of the French Mayor, Charles Dutheil. Glossop was twinned with the French town of Millau. Many of the town's children had pen friends in Millau and were encouraged to speak and write the language on exchange visits. In July 1957 Mayor Claude Woolley and the Town Clerk Colin Campbell had visited France and were welcomed with the banner 'Honneur à la Ville de Glossop'

February 1958. The town was again hit by blizzards but these ladies still have the shopping to do. The picture is looking towards Victoria Street through the archway at the side of the Norfolk Arms. The Norfolk Arms was first called the Tontine, and was built as a coaching Inn on the Turnpike Road. The Royal Mail coach to Manchester, *The Umpire* from Sheffield and *The Regulator* all stopped at the Norfolk Arms in the 1800's.

Mayor of Millau Charles Dutheil (centre) with members of the local town twinning committee. A new Twinning Committee was set up in 1984 and three years later the town was twinned with Bad Vilbel in Germany.

Exchange visits took place between students in both countries and here we see French students from Millau who came to stay with Grammar School pupils in 1961. Many life long friendships were formed through these exchanges. With the students are French teachers Mr. Fred Davies and Miss Gladys Wanklin, outside the school.

August 1958. Excavations were started at Melandra. The dig was led by Dr. J. Petch of Woodford and members of Mottram and Broadbottom WEA assisted. Here we see the foundation stones of the Castle which were revealed. Melandra Castle was built c. AD 79 and was called Edrotalia by the Romans. It was first discovered in 1771 by Reverend John Watson, a rector from Stockport. In June 1994 a team of archaeologists from Manchester University excavated the bath block of the castle and found fragments of bowls, jugs, tiles and cooking pots. Vandals soon filled in the trenches that showed cobbled floors after the teams left. Often the teams have to repair damage before they can start new digs in the castle.

1958

In October 1957 first year pupils from the Grammar School were taken to Melandra Castle by their history teacher, Mr. Scott.

September 1958. Chunal Lane before it was widened in September 1959. The photograph is taken from Hague Street, Whitfield and shows the dangerous bends where many accidents had occurred. The road was first constructed in 1795 for travellers from Chapel-en-le-Frith to Enterclough, an area now submerged under the Longdendale reservoirs.

October 1958. The Abbot's Chair is situated on Monks Road which runs from near the Grouse Inn to Charlesworth along Whiteley Nab seen in the distance in the picture above. The chair is said to have been the site where rents of the Glossop Estate were collected when in the possession of the Abbots of Basingwerke, North Wales. The Monks were of the Cistercian Order and the chair probably dated from the 14th century.

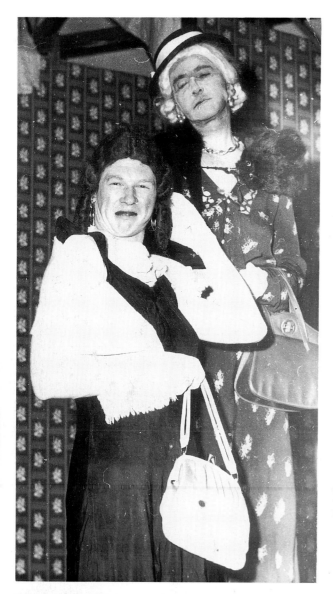

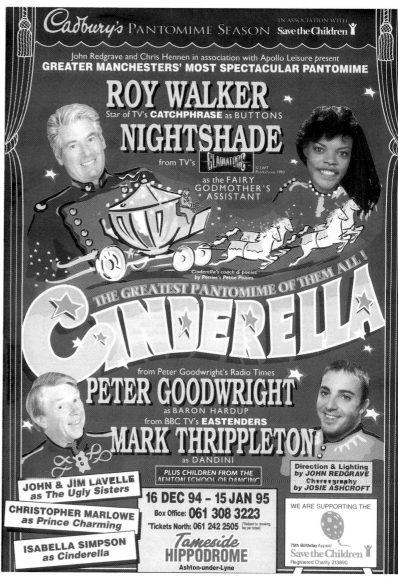

October 1958. Peter Goodwright, the impersonator from Glossop who has appeared on stage, screen and radio, was here impersonating Hilda Baker, as part of the entertainment at a Hot Pot supper for the town's old folk during Old Folks Week. In 1994 he appeared in Cinderella at Tameside Hippodrome as Baron Hardup. Peter was originally a cashier at Barclays Bank and is now based at Salisbury. He attended the Grammar School and was a keen actor in amateur dramatics. He left the bank in 1958 to be a part of a Manchester Playhouse production that was broadcast on the radio. That led to 'Worker's Playtime' and many more offers of work.

February 1959. A Bronze Age urn was found on the south side of Shire Hill during the building of bungalow for councillor Gordon Hurst, seen in the photograph with Tom Haynes. It contained only bone dust. A coin of Constantine II marked Augustus 337-340 AD was also found on the same site.

1959. Church Street South, Old Glossop, known to locals as Chris's Brow and Woodhouses Brow. Six houses dating from the 17th century are still standing and are quite rightly listed buildings. Their dates and initials appear over the doors and they have stone mullioned windows. At one time it was thought that Canon Fauval (whose name lives on in Fauval Road) converted one into a school. In 1949 these houses were featured in the film 'Cure for Love' starring Robert Donat. Plaster casts were taken of the walls, to get an exact copy for studio sets. In October 1994 it was proposed by Highway Chiefs and local councillors to ban traffic from Church Street South between the Bull pub and the Old Cross or the Queen's. It would allow tourists to view the Old Cross and the 17th century cottages.

1959

1959. The Saxon Cross at Old Glossop. It was here that the annual fair and weekly markets took place from 1289-1833. Kings and queens have been proclaimed here and the stocks and pinfold used to be nearby. In 1910 the cross was moved away from the cottage bearing the name 'Old Cross', to its more central position in the square and the top was added to the cross shaft. After the Market Act of 1844, the 13th Duke of Norfolk built the Market Hall near the Town Hall and the markets were transferred from Old Glossop. The Parish Church in the background dates from Norman times. It was rebuilt in 1831 and additions to it were completed in 1923. The nave was built in 1914 and the vicar of All Saints, Father Fred Whitehead, held a service to celebrate its 80th anniversary in November 1994. Earlier in 1994, two stained glass windows were installed. The coat-of-arms of the 13th Duke of Norfolk, as well as those of Lichfield, Southwell and Derby, being the three diocese that the church had been in over the years. The glass panels show some early history of buildings still around the town as well as weavers, railway and steam power.

1959

March 1959. The Town's W V S (Women's Voluntary Service) supplied gallons of soup and tea to rescue workers, when a potholer, Neil Moss, was trapped in the Devil's Pothole in the Peak Cavern in Buxton. The W.V.S. was founded in the U.K. in 1938 and was designated 'Royal' in 1966. In the war they helped lessen the disruptions and in peacetime they supplement the social services. In 1944 they pioneered the first home-help services. The WRVS run meals-on-wheels and provide voluntary workers for day centres, hospitals and playgroups and also provide a prison visiting service.

September 1959. Littlemoor Sunday School Rose Queen Rosemary Bradbury. The Independent Chapel on Victoria Street, was founded in 1811 by the Kershaws, mill owners of Whitfield, the area then being called Little Moor. Many churches held rose queen festivals as a way of involving children in the fund raising activities of the church or chapel. Every little girl longed to dress up and be chosen to be in the procession. Mothers spent weeks in preparation so that the children looked their best and sometimes there was jealousy in some places if a child wasn't picked. Many groups wisely chose on the merit of those with the best attendance records in the Sunday School. The building was turned into a theatre club in the late 1960's and was later used by Richard North to manufacture sportswear. An amateur local actor wants to turn the building into a live theatre.

1959

November 1959. Bank House on Henry Street was once the District Bank. Here the bank safe is being removed. The building is now Glossop Heritage Centre and contains a wealth of historical artifacts and memorabilia. There are always new displays and things to buy. Coffee is available in a Victorian setting and the voluntary staff are always very helpful. The building to the right, now a restaurant, was once a carpet shop owned by Froggats. The building behind the crane is the Conservative Club on Norfolk Street.

The Telephone Exchange was being built here and was opened in February 1960 by the Mayor Samuel Bamford. All telephone calls could be made automatically, without the need to go via the operator. The double-decker bus on the market ground was the No.127 to Hadfield, via Newshaw Lane. The Town Hall was built in 1838 by Bernard Edward Howard, Lord of the Manor and the 12th Duke of Norfolk. At the time of this picture the building had not been cleaned. In 1976 the present Duke of Norfolk unveiled a plaque in the front entrance to the Market Hall to celebrate the restoration of the Town Hall to its original appearance without shops in the side streets. Before 1838 the site of the Town Hall and Market ground was a field called the Platt. It belonged to the landlord of the Norfolk Arms then called the Tontine.

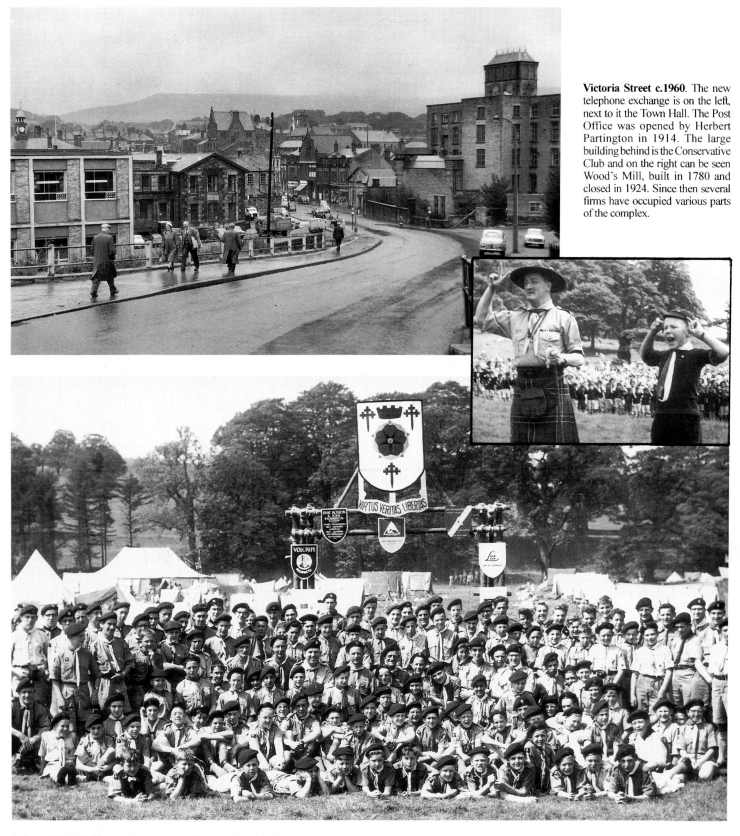

Victoria Street c.1960. The new telephone exchange is on the left, next to it the Town Hall. The Post Office was opened by Herbert Partington in 1914. The large building behind is the Conservative Club and on the right can be seen Wood's Mill, built in 1780 and closed in 1924. Since then several firms have occupied various parts of the complex.

In June 1960 146 Glossop Scouts went to Chatsworth to join in the Scout, Cub, Guide and Brownie Jamboree. It was a rally with 2800 scouts and 1800 guides attending from all over the world. The Chief Scout was Sir Charles MacLean and local cub, Trevor Howard, took the 'Grand Howl'. Under the Glossop Coat-of-Arms are shields from some of the town's factories. Volcrepe products, Isaac Jackson & Sons (Fasteners) Ltd., Lux Lux Underwear, Levi Jackson & Sons, Flexy Brushes Ltd. and others covered up by the large group in the picture.

April 1960. **The Royale**. The Melandra Field group dug on the Royale hoping to find the continuation of Doctor's Gate, the Roman road which stretches from the Snake road and ends abruptly in Old Glossop. They believed the road led from Old Glossop across the Royale and High Street East to Cross Cliffe Road. The group dug for several hours and were led by Mr J. Hodgson of Withington, and Dr J.W. Jackson, a geologist from Manchester Museum. The only find was a clay pipe.

1960

10 May 1960 saw the official opening of the new Grammar School on Talbot Road. A painting was donated to the school by Mottram artist L.S. Lowry, who can be seen on the right of the picture. Professor W. Mansfield Cooper, who performed the opening ceremony, is on the left.

During the same month a terracotta mural was unveiled at the school. The theme of the mural is adolescent education. It is the work of ex. pupil David Metcalf and his wife. Headmaster Mr. Lord is seen here beside the mural.

1960

June 1960. High Street West. The scene of an accident between a motor cyclist and a Hillman car near the corner of Market Street. The Newmarket Hotel and Burgons are on the corner.

November 1960. The Queen of Glossop's Charm School being chosen at the Victoria Hall. She was Mrs. Elizabeth Allan of Charlesworth (second-left). The panel of judges were Mrs. Gibbs (Mayoress), Shiela Buxton (singer), Roger Moffatt, Eileen Sladin and Mr. & Mrs. Max Wibberley. The singer Shiela Buxton, next to the Mayoress, was known as Manchester's 'Little Miss Music' after the television show she hosted in the sixties. She was the feature singer with the Northern Dance Orchestra, participated in three Royal Command performances and had her own radio show, 'Make Way for Music'. Originally from Ashton she retired to Malta, dying in March 1994 at the age of 62.

March 1961. Jo Grimmond, Liberal MP representing Orkney and Shetland for 33 years, visited Glossop when campaigning for the party. In 1964 he again visited Derbyshire to attend meetings in Whaley Bridge and Chapel. He died at the age of 80 in October 1993.

June 1961. Bill Grundy, presenter of television's 'People and Faces' is seen here crowning Marion Longston as the new 'Charm Queen' during a fancy dress ball at the Victoria Hall, held in aid of the Mayor's charities. The ball was held on midsummer's Eve and several contestants dressed up as St.Trinian's girls.

1961

June 1961. Signing autographs at the Red Court Garden Fête were members of the cast of Granada Television's Coronation Street - Pat Phoenix (Elsie Tanner), Anne Cunningham (Linda Cheveski) and Ernest Walder (Ivan Cheveski) who played the parts of Elsie Tanner's daughter and son-in-law in the series.

Back Kershaw Street. c.1961. Both streets were demolished as part of the town's slum clearance plan. Many rows of houses were built by men who then chose to live in the finest one, usually the end house and the new street took on that person's name. Most streets were named in 1876 and include Talbot Road and Talbot Street after John Talbot, vicar from 1494-1535; Philip Howard Road after St.Philip Howard, a Catholic traitor who died in the Tower in 1595; Ellison Street after Matthew Ellison, the Duke of Norfolk's local land agent; Kershaw Street after the family who founded Littlemoor Chapel, and Fitzalan Street after Henry Fitzalen-Howard, the 15th Duke of Norfolk. During the cotton famine of 1862-4 many new roads were constructed to create work for the unemployed. Hall Meadow, Fauvel, Dinting and North Road are examples from this period.

1961

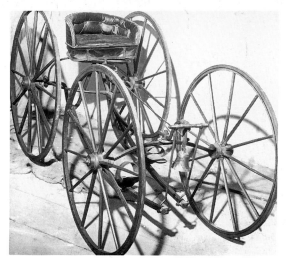

This four wheeled cycle was found in the attic of a confectioner's shop in 1961. It was thought to be over 100 years old. In fact, it could have been far earlier as records reveal that a Reigate schoolmaster built a four-wheeled *'travelling chaise without horses,* which was propelled by foot power applied to a cranked axle as early as 1760.

April 1962. The Market steps were considered too dangerous as people stepped straight onto Market Street into traffic, and so the local council considered closure. The Market Hall was built in 1844 by the 13th Duke of Norfolk.

1962

In 1962 the Mayor was Earnest Farmer, seen here with his wife and their son and daughter and grandchildren Susan Farmer and Graham Hadfield.

1962

June 1962. Mr W.E. Sowerbutts - Bill - the famous gardener, opened Simmondley Garden Party, which raised £100 for the Freedom From Hunger campaign. Bill often featured in the radio programme 'Gardeners' Question Time'. He lived in the Lodge of the former Etherow House, opposite Millbrook House in Tintwistle.

August 1962. Dinting Junior Cricket Team won the Glossop league championships for the second year. On the front row, from the left, are:
T. Porter, J. Ash, P. Bates, H. Elliott (Captain), J. Hall and K. Wilde.

December 1962. Florrie Lindley (Betty Alberge), who ran the corner shop in 'Coronation Street', attended a concert in the Town Hall in aid of Oxfam. The Oxford Committee for Famine Relief was founded in 1942 to alleviate poverty and distress throughout the world. Most of the funds go towards providing long term development aid to third world countries. The three world theory divides our planet thus: 1st World - developing capitalist economies. 2nd World - developed Communist countries. 3rd World - under-developed countries.

May 1963. Jack Callaghan of Simmondley celebrated 25 years as an A.A. patrolman. The Automobile Association began in 1905 and grew out of an organisation which provided cyclist patrols to warn motorists of police speed traps. The speed limit was 12 mph at that time! From 1906 the patrolmen were expected to salute all members displaying the A.A. badge. This practice was discontinued in 1960 to promote better road safety, but the association's motto, "Courtesy and Care" was still upheld. In 1963 there were three million members and the badge incorporated the wings of the Motor Union, which had amalgamated with the A.A. in 1910. The bike in the picture was purchased from BSA in March 1960 and was one of a batch numbered YUC 501-760. It is a 600cc M21 and incorporates tank mudguards, a windscreen, leg guards and fairings to protect the rider. The motor cycle combination was first used in 1919. Two-way radios were fitted in 1952. In addition to vans the A.A. still use motorbike patrols today.

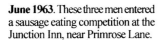

June 1963. These three men entered a sausage eating competition at the Junction Inn, near Primrose Lane.

The Victoria Hall and Library in 1963. Built in 1887 on land belonging to Baron Howard, with donations to mark Queen Victoria's Jubilee celebrations, Edward Partington, who became Lord Doverdale and owned Turn Lee paper mill, and Herbert Rhodes, whose families founded Mersey Mills, each donated £2,000. The foundation stones were laid in July 1887 and two stone tablets on either side of the library door, commemorate these benefactors and honour their generosity.

1963

Howard Park and Wood's Baths in 1963. These were the Jubilee gift of the Wood family in 1887. The 12 acre park cost £6,000 to lay out and was funded by Mrs. Anne Kershaw Wood and her husband, Samuel, and brother-in-law Daniel Wood, who also jointly bore the cost of the swimming baths and hospital. In 1956 Councillor Harry Cooper was chairman of the Baths, Parks and Cemeteries Committee. In November 1961 the tenancy of the gate cottage (left) went to a Sister at the hospital. There is an Ice Age boulder in the park that is between fifty thousand and seven hundred thousand years old. In November 1994 High Peak Council decided that there were too many ducks on the pond and stopped feeding them. It was felt that discouraging visitors from feeding them would regulate the numbers, but, as one parent pointed out, the squawking of hungry ducks was nothing compared to the sound of a child who has just been told that he can never feed the ducks again!

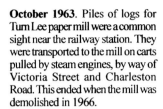

October 1963. Piles of logs for Turn Lee paper mill were a common sight near the railway station. They were transported to the mill on carts pulled by steam engines, by way of Victoria Street and Charleston Road. This ended when the mill was demolished in 1966.

January 1964. The streets bordering Norfolk Square bear the names of the Howard family - Henry, Edward and Bernard. Houses on Bernard and Edward Streets were demolished and the site turned into a car park. This picture shows Edward Street from Arundel Street. Below, the corner shop on Bernard Street remains. On all main roads the street lamps reached to the height of the gutters. On the side roads they were not so high.

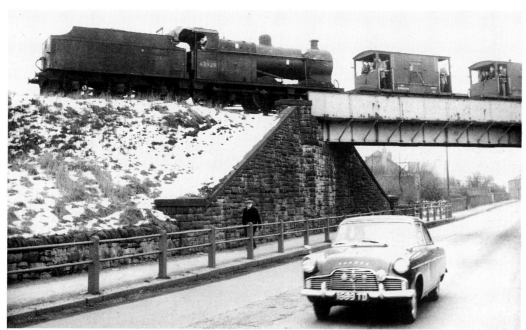

The Melandra railway bridge at Brookfield. The last freight train passed over this bridge in February 1964. The line ran from Dinting to Waterside mill, a distance of two miles. The line was constructed to deliver raw materials and coal to the local mills and to collect finished articles. The bridge was pulled down in 1966.

1964

April 1964 The opening of the sewage works at Melandra. The opening ceremony was performed by Alderman H. Turner (Bert), the Mayor.

September 1964. Frederick (Freddy) Sewards Trueman played in a benefit match at the North Road cricket ground. To the delight of the large crowd he hit 70 runs. Born in Stainton, Yorkshire, Trueman became an apprentice brick-layer before developing into the first genuinely fast bowler in post war English cricket. He played for Yorkshire for 19 years from 1949 to 1968, participating in 67 Tests and taking 307 wickets between 1952 and 1965. In a first class career he took 2,304 wickets and made three centuries. In his forthright Yorkshire style he has worked as a cricket writer and commentator since his retirement from the game. He was awarded the OBE in 1989.

1964

October 1964. George Alfred Brown, vice chairman and deputy leader of the Labour Party from 1960, speaking on the Market ground. Born at Southwark, London, in 1914, he was an official of the Transport & General Worker's Union before entering Parliament as MP for Belper in 1945. Brown supported Hugh Gaitskell in opposing unilateral disarmament when opposition spokesman on defence. He successfully contested Harold Wilson for the party leadership in 1963. A flamboyant, impetuous and controversial figure, George Brown was awarded a life peerage after losing his seat in 1970. He died in 1985.

January 1965. Mr. Frank Dearnaley, the works manager of Hawkeshead Mills, which was built in 1791 by James Starkie, as a cotton spinning mill near the Shire Hill area. Glossop once had two cinemas; The Palace on Chapel Street, demolished in 1959, and the Empire on High Street West which closed in 1962. Mr Dearnaley decided to operate his own cinema in the factory. The first film show in Britain was held in a hall in London in 1896. The cinematograph used had been invented in France the previous year by the Lumiére brothers. It was both a camera and a projector and held only 50 feet of film, which lasted for some 45 seconds. People thronged to the Music Halls to see these 'photographs that moved', but after a while the novelty waned and the films were put on at the end of the evening to clear the hall. For this reason they became known as 'chasers'. The cinema was saved by fairground men, who showed films in tents in country areas. By this time films lasted for up to 15 minutes and by 1906 many venues had plush seats and electric organs. Permanent cinemas began to spring up in shops in the towns. By 1914 these had been replaced by 'Picture Palaces'. As the films were quite scratched and flickered they were known as 'the flicks'. By 1927 sound had been added to the films and they became known as 'the talkies'. By 1950 television began to compete with the cinemas, stealing their audience. The industry tried to fight back, firstly with innovative 3D films viewed through special glasses, followed by the wide screen of Cinemascope and the Glorious Technicolour. By the sixties the weekly figures for cinema audiences had plummeted from 25 million to 4 million, forcing the closure of many small cinemas, including Glossop's Palace and Empire.

1965

April 1965. The Wesley Methodist Chapel on High Street West was demolished after 125 years. It was closed under a local Methodist reorganisation scheme, when it was decided to build a new chapel round the corner. The new chapel was built in 1966.

Wesley Methodist's Chapel from the outside, with Don Jones' newsagents, where the Daily Mail was still only 3d! After the war newsprint production was 42% lower than it had been

The new Central Methodist Chapel and the Health Centre were built in 1966 on the land where Shepley Mill had once stood. In January 1995 the 29 year old church was facing a repair and improvement bill of £50,000. The first Health Centre, built under the National Health Service, opened in Bristol in 1954. These centres helped to lower the infant mortality rate. At the beginning of the century the infant death rate stood at 150 per thousand live births but by 1951 that figure had fallen to 29 and by 1980 only 11 deaths per thousand were recorded. This photograph, taken from the bridge off George Street, shows the gas towers on Arundel Street. The gas works closed in April 1957 and Glossop was then supplied by Denton works. Gas could be made cheaper by the development of larger grid systems, rendering small works obsolete. On the left hand side of the bridge is Harehills Park, known locally as the Sandholes. The park was gifted to the townspeople in 1921 by Francis Edward Howard as a memorial to his son, Philip, and to all those from Glossop who had died in the First World War. In 1994 trees were cut down and bulbs planted. The following year the paths alongside the river were resurfaced and seats provided. Future plans include improvement of the play area and the addition of new lighting and signs to other beauty spots, to help tourists to get the best from the town.

1966

September 1963. The Plough Inn, Dinting, was flooded, forcing the licensee, Miss Ethel Mary Pooler and her 73 year old mother to find the only dry place to sit. The Plough had been a stopping point for the mail coach as it travelled through the town when the road outside was very narrow. The pub was extended by knocking down the two adjoining cottages. The plough above the door was put up by licensees Colin and Lilian Campbell in 1976.

November 1965. Armistice Day Parade. The Territorial Army, a reserve force of trained men for use in an emergency, marched down Norfolk Street. In 1914 the T.A. Drill Hall was on Glossop market ground. The Home Guard was disbanded in Britain in 1957. Originally formed as Local Defence Volunteers in 1940 and then disbanded after the Second World War, the force was reformed in 1952 at the time of the Korean War.

Glossop Council 1965-66. The Mayor was Donald Joseph Clement Moore, a great lover of football and a boyhood friend of Granada television's Stuart Hall. Donald Moore's father, Joe Moore, was the manager of Hadfield's Picture Drome. Councillor Moore died in May 1994. The Town Clerk in this picture is D.E. Smith.

1965/66

September 1966 saw the centenary of Glossop becoming a Municipal Borough. The Charter had arrived at the railway station in 1866. This photograph shows a very happy council in the Chambers on Centenary Day. The Mayor was Mrs. Ada Williams, the third lady mayor in the town's history. The first was Mrs. Mary Partington in 1916, the second Mrs. May Louise Casey in 1950. In January 1994 the Charter was stolen from a glass case on the first floor of the Town Hall.

October 1966. During the Centenary celebrations a revival of the Rush Cart and Well Dressing ceremonies took place at Whitfield. Mr. W. Carter dressed the Rush Cart and prepared the horse for the procession. The top picture was taken near the library. The Rush Cart procession was organised by Whitfield Youth Centre and was attended by over ten thousand people. There was an Ox Roast on the market ground, in the town centre, as there had been in 1902 to celebrate the coronation of Edward VII. At the Well Dressing, **below**, a service of thanksgiving for the water was conducted and over £60 was collected in the wells. The festival was revived in 1985, when colourful floats and Carnival Queens passed through the town to Whitfield. This tradition was again revived in September 1995. In November 1994 a well was discovered in a house in Victoria Street when the footings were being dug for an extension. The house dated from 1820.

Margot Bryant, alias Coronation Street's Minnie Coldwell, famous for her role with Bobby the cat, is seen here signing autographs at a fund raising day on behalf of the Cat's Protection League.

1967

February 1967. A wall painting was discovered at the Station Hotel, Norfolk Street, during the redecoration of the concert room. The murals, painted in oils c.1853, covered four walls and thought to be the work of J.G. Day. Mr Albert Garnett, the landlord, thought that the murals had been painted before the building became a public house, possibly when it was a meeting room attended by Lord Howard of the Manor.

February 1967. Stuart Hall, popular local star of radio and television, was visiting the Town Hall to compère a fashion show organised by the Family Planning Association. Mayor Ada Williams is next to Stuart's wife, Hazel. The models were Carol Dunning, Jennifer Lowe, Maxine Turner, Judy Moss, Anita Harris and Patsy Bibberfield.

C.1970. Glossop Band led the British Legion Parade to Manor Park. Chief Inspector Ernest Bennett, Inspector Terry Corrigan and Sergeant Ken Simpson walked in front of the band. In 1880 there were three local bands in existence; The Borough, The Old and The Reed. The Band Room in Wood Street was built by the Partingtons, who supplied the uniforms.

1974. Artist L.S. Lowry attends an art exhibition at the Centre, organised by Mr Dunsmore, left, with Councillor Chatterton, right, L.S. Lowry was a frequent visitor to Glossop, living in nearby Mottram. Each week he partook of a salad at Lord's Café on High Street West.

1974 The National Westminster Bank and Norfolk Square.

1974. Enthusiastic members of Glossop Centre's Art Class pose on the steps in Talbot Street for fellow class member Harry Buxton. The Centre for adult Education was built in 1899 for the education of bright children. The Technical school opened in 1901 with thirty pupils and became a Grammar School in 1902. By 1959 it was in use as an annexe for West End Secondary Modern School and became the Adult Education Centre in 1966.

1973-4 The last Borough Council at Glossop before joining High peak. A civic dinner was held to mark the end of an era. The Mayor was George Chatterton. Some members of the council at the time were Ada Williams and Messrs. Partridge, Bredbury, Jefferson, Duggan, Turner and Buxton. The Town Clerk was Mr. D.G. Hodgkinson. In 1994 the local government commission had plans to carve up Derbyshire but High peak was to survive, along with Amber Valley, Derbyshire Dales, Erewash and South Derbyshire.

1972-3. The Mayor, Fred Thomasson with his wife, Dorothy.

George Chatterton was Glossop's last Mayor in 1973-4. He died in February 1988 at the age of 72.